EXPLORING
Historic Wailuku

EXPLORING
Historic Wailuku

George Engebretson

Design by
Gonzalez Design Company

Exploring Historic Wailuku is an ongoing
community effort. Readers with additional
information about any of the photos or
captions in this book are invited to contact
the publisher at the mailing address or
e-mail below.

Watermark Publishing
1000 Bishop Street, Suite 501-A
Honolulu, HI 96813
Telephone (808) 587-7766
www.watermarkpublishing.net
e-mail: sales@watermarkpublishing.net

Library of Congress Control Number: 99-133727
ISBN 0-9631154-3-X

Printed in China

Contents

Acknowledgments

Creating such a diverse collection of photographs and memories was made possible by the cooperation and generosity of the people of Wailuku — the families, companies, service organizations and government agencies who make up this vibrant, historic community.

Many thanks to Cathy Riley, Gail Burns and Beryl Bal of the Maui Historical Society; Janice and Tom Fairbanks of the Old Wailuku Inn at Ulupono; Avery Chumbley and Clayton Suzuki of Wailuku Agribusiness; Fred Araki of Iao Congregational Church; Irvin Yamada of Photography by Irvin; retired *Maui News* photographer Wayne Tanaka; and preservation advocate Barbara Long. *Mahalo* also to Yuklin Aluli, Reynolds Burkland, Wendy Hanada Choi, Elmer Cravalho, Linda Decker, Debbie Doyle, Manuel Duarte, George Emura, Father Marvin Fultz, Connie Garcia, Sammy Garcia, Yukuo Hanada, Doris Hotta, Susanne Hotta, Diana Hutchinson, Robert and Lisa Joslin, Faye Kashiwa, George Kaya, Catherine Nobriga Kim, Rev. Robb Kojima, Mike Lyons, Sara Medeiros, Domingo Molina, Henry Molina, Michael Munekiyo, Seiji Muraoka, Joe Myhand, Pat Nitta, Mike Nobriga, Stanley Okamoto, August Percha, Janice Pruett, Adelaide Rowland, Pat Saka, Mitzi Sakamoto, Phyllis Sato, Yoshie Sato, Ed Silva, Beverly Stanich, Jonathan Starr, Jimmy Takamiya, Robert Kimura, Elaine Kato Tamasaka, Cathy Toda, Yukioshi Yoda, Florence Yonemoto, Sandy Yoshimori and all the others who shared the spirit of Wailuku with the author and researchers.

A very special thanks to Maui County Mayor James "Kimo" Apana, to County Economic Development Coordinator Rosalyn H. Baker, and to County Economic Development Specialist Yuki Lei Sugimura, who paved the way for *Exploring Historic Wailuku*.

Foreword

The historic town of Wailuku is much more than just the seat of government for Maui County. Those fortunate enough to live and work here know it as a hometown of quiet neighborhoods, friendly people and happy memories.

For me, Wailuku is the place where my grandfather launched the salvage business everyone calls the Apana Junkyard, where my father started his nursery on the outskirts of town, where one auntie ran an appliance store and another a dress shop across the street from Nakagawa Tailor — my wife's family business. It's a place where the shopkeepers still call you by name, and where the flavors of Asia and the Pacific come together in the bento you can buy at a mom-and-pop *okazu-ya*.

Folks who call Wailuku home have lots of wonderful stories to tell about life in this one-time plantation town. Maybe that's why historic preservation is such an important priority for residents, business people and all of us in County government.

Exploring Historic Wailuku provides a lasting overview of our town's rich heritage and proud civic tradition. These priceless pictures, many of them tucked away for years in family photo albums, capture the essence of Wailuku as it was — and what it can be again.

As we continue to preserve the best of yesterday's Wailuku — and incorporate its spirit into our plans for the future — I invite you to discover for yourself the historic streets and charming buildings of old Wailuku town.

Aloha,

James "Kimo" Apana
Mayor, County of Maui

Introduction

Wailuku, Maui, is the classic American small town. With roots deep in Hawaiian history, it is also a small town with a tropical twist — fringed with sugar cane, washed by tradewinds, located just a short, scenic drive from windsurfing meccas and swank beach resorts.

But for all its South Seas charm, Wailuku is still Anytown, USA — a tidy landscape of trim storefronts and manicured lawns, shady avenues and green ballparks, old stone schoolhouses and churches of every stripe. Wailuku is the kind of place where neighborhoods still feel like neighborhoods, where mom-and-pop stores are passed along down the generations, where stately public buildings buzz with the nuts-and-bolts business of local government.

Forged in a crucible of native and immigrant cultures, framed by misty valleys steeped in island lore, Wailuku is also a place with a rich, romantic history. Before the booming sugar industry made it a model plantation town, Wailuku was a favorite of Hawaii's kings and commoners. When the first Westerners arrived in the late 18th Century, the area was home to a large community of Hawaiians who planted great tracts of taro and fished the waters of the near-by Pacific. From his home base at today's Wailuku Civic Center, Maui's powerful chief Kahekili launched successful canoe invasions of neighboring islands and fought bloody battles in the near reaches of 'Iao Valley. By the Battle of Kepaniwai in 1790, when the bodies of fallen warriors dammed 'Iao Stream, the area was known as *Wai-luku* — "water of destruction."

In 1837 the *ali'i* granted land rights for a Christian mission adjacent to the royal compound, and by mid-century the first sugar plantation had taken root, luring a new wave of settlers to run the mills and work the fields. As sugar cane blossomed, so did Wailuku's population, from 4,000 in the 1860s to 8,000 by the turn of the century. Served by a good seaport at nearby Kahului, Wailuku quickly eclipsed the old Hawaiian capital of Lahaina as the island's nerve center; in 1905 it was named the seat of government of newly formed Maui County.

Soon came all the trappings of the successful small town: a public library and a pillared courthouse, genteel homes and auto dealers. The business district mushroomed with restaurants and banks, theaters and saloons, hotels and markets. As the years passed, old establishments closed and new ones opened, usually in the same buildings. Cobblers and blacksmiths gave way to jewelers and dry cleaners, which in turn gave way to art galleries and boutiques. And still the old buildings stood proudly along the sidewalks of Main and Market and Vineyard.

The pace of progress slowed for Wailuku in the 1960s, '70s and '80s. New malls and bedroom communities opened in nearby Kahului. Wailuku Sugar Co. closed its century-old mill operation. Hawaii's red-hot visitor industry turned the spotlight toward the sunny beach communities on Maui's lee shores. As a sign of the times, some of Wailuku's historic buildings were razed to make way for gas stations and convenience stores, while others were simply closed and shuttered.

Today, this historic town is enjoying a groundswell of rehabilitation and renewal. County government has taken the lead in renovating sites like the old stone courthouse and the original, Mediterranean-style County office building. Community groups and private enterprise join forces for the study and implementation of historic preservation. Artisans and white-collar professionals hang out their shingles at refurbished shops and plantation homes. And commercial real estate developers are creating new retail and office space — giving facelifts to fading buildings, retaining old facades and foundations, and, most important, helping rekindle the civic spirit of old Wailuku town.

Likewise, *Exploring Historic Wailuku* is both a celebration of the past and a hopeful look ahead. This photographic history is an interactive guide to many of the town's homes and businesses, schools and churches, community centers and public buildings. For those structures still standing, it is a nostalgic glimpse of these buildings in their heyday — when politicians made speeches from Iao Theater's street-side balcony, and shoppers from all over the island bought penny candy at the Kress store. For those buildings that are no more, their photos offer a refresher course on some true Wailuku institutions: Town Hall, Home Furnishings, the Maui Grand Hotel and others.

Each of these photographs is keyed to the gate-fold map at the back of the book. Those who follow its route will find the soul of old Wailuku in a quiet neighborhood, in an old plantation store, in the graceful architectural touches still evident along Market Street. For visitors to Maui, this Wailuku walking map offers a behind-the-scenes look at an island treasure, tucked away off the tourist track. For residents, it is a reminder of a rich heritage, a reaffirmation of the spirit — and the promise — of Maui's quintessential small town.

Wide-Open Wailuku

Sugar was still spreading its roots ca. 1915, when fields of billowing cane nearly surrounded a fast-growing Wailuku. Here the towers of Wailuku Union Church and Ka'ahumanu Church rise prominently at left and left center, while new commercial buildings proliferate along Main Street at right center. Kahului Railroad's Wailuku Depot stands front and center.

Maui Historical Society

CHAPTER ONE
Sugar Town

Field Workers

Laborers level terraces to plant cane on sloping acreage outside of town. Wailuku Sugar Co. was organized
in 1862, when the plantation employed primarily Hawaiians and contract laborers newly arrived from China. By 1886,
according to company records, the work force included 123 Portuguese, 107 Hawaiians, 16 South Pacific islanders,
ten Chinese, nine Americans and four Norwegians. Later came Manchurians in 1897, Spaniards in 1898,
African-Americans in 1901, Koreans in 1903 and Filipinos in 1906. *Wailuku Agribusiness*

Wailuku 1920
An early aerial photograph shows a model American small town, its tidy streets lined with stately
public buildings, bustling businesses and homes with mature trees and well-tended lawns. The heart of Wailuku
is anchored here by Ka'ahumanu Church and the still-new Wailuku Civic Center buildings (*upper left*)
and the Wailuku Depot at lower right. *Iao Congregational Church*

The King's Rules for "Acre Persons"

The cane shall be hewed by the sugar planters so that their sugar can be cooked and shall bring it to the place where the carts must go. Then it shall be for the king's carts to go after it together with the one who owns the cane, and he is to load it on the cart, and the bullock driver shall take it to the mill. The cane owner shall keep the bullock driver in food...

Here is this concerning the luna. From this time Kuhikeelani is the Luna to those that plant by the acre. This is his duty. He shall look after the cane properly and shall do what he can to make it a success and he shall teach the planters so that they will do their planting properly and their caring for same. And should they not take care, according to the document, then it must be the luna who is to punish them according to the agreement. And he shall do his work in a proper manner as the luna should do.

Here is this. If the luna should direct the men the proper way and some should disobey the luna in his proper direction, according to what is agreed upon in the document then that person is to be tried and if the disobedience is through being lazy, or not wanting to obey, then that person shall be removed from the acre.

Here is this. The acres which have not been cultivated shall be immediately cultivated by the men from this day until the last day of November, then finish. And should any person not plant immediately they shall be punished as follows: If there be a half acre left, he shall go to work for the king some half of the year; and if one quarter of an acre is left then he shall go to work for the king some quarter of the year.

— Rules for independent growers supplying cane to the king's sugar mill, signed by Kamehameha III, September 1840 (translated from Hawaiian)

59 Market Street Sugar Mill

In 1865 Wailuku Sugar's first mill in Wailuku town replaced a livery stable west of Market, on a site stretching about 300 yards south of 'Iao Stream. Upon its completion the mill's tall stack and water wheel proved to be something of a visitor attraction. Earlier, this location had been the site of the sugar mill built and operated by Kamehameha III. Here the mill stack appears sometime after the turn of the century, just prior to its demolition.
Wailuku Agribusiness

9

62 Pu'uohala Camp

Wailuku Sugar Co. workers were housed primarily in neat rows of wood-frame houses like these at Pu'uohala Camp. Today Pu'uohala is a rural neighborhood of private homes tucked away at the north edge of town, just past the Happy Valley area.
Maui Historical Society

⚅ Wailuku Sugar Company Mill

When Wailuku Sugar's second mill in Wailuku town was built in the late 1880s, raw cane was hauled to the site by ox carts and a pair of mule teams. In 1906 this mill made way for a new $400,000 facility on the same site, which operated until 1978. That mill was razed in the mid-'80s to make way for the Millyard office and residential subdivision. Today the Wailuku Post Office is located where the sugar mill once stood. *Hawai'i State Archives*

10 Maui News

The *Maui News* printed its first issue in 1900 and continues to publish today. The paper's first office was in this small building adjacent to Ka'ahumanu Church. All that remains today is the low retaining wall; the *News'* first home is now Honoli'i Park on the southwest corner of Main and High, next to the church graveyard. In the late 18th Century, this area was the site of the home and *heiau* of the powerful chief Kahekili and his family.

Maui News/Maui Historical Society

CHAPTER TWO
Markets and Merchants

14

🄳 Maui Hotel

The Maui Hotel was opened in 1901 by Oʻahu transplant W.H. Field, owner of Home Bakery in Honolulu, who ran it as a full-service hotel until he leased the nearby Maui Grand in 1923. Located on the northwest corner of Main and High, the inn served as a base camp for travelers en route to Haleakalā or into ʻĪao Valley. Management also built a rustic annex in the valley called Kapaniwai. The *Maui News* building appears at the intersection's southwest corner (*left*). *Ray Jerome Baker Collection/Bishop Museum*

20 Maui Hotel

The inn doubled as Wailuku's first modern drug store, with state-of-the-art pharmaceuticals shipped in from San Francisco. In 1927 Haleakala Motors opened at the location after extensive renovations to the old hotel building. This new layout with improved setbacks and visibility, the *Maui News* editorialized, greatly improved what had been "the most dangerous corner on Maui." In 1941 the building was demolished for a new auto showroom. Today the corner is the site of the One Main Plaza office building. *Maui Historical Society*

21 Wailuku Hotel
This three-story structure hosted both travelers and residents near the northeast corner of Main and High. In 1938 management renovated an old radio and electronic shop next door and added the Cocktail Gardens, a tropical restaurant and dance pavilion complete with hanging vines, potted palms and concealed lighting, where patrons could cut a rug every Saturday night. The hotel is shown here approximately ten years before it was remodeled in 1970 to become part of the new Maui Medical Group. *Wayne Tanaka Collection*

16 **Vineyard Tavern**
Property owner Masato "Charlie" Yonemoto stands before the Vineyard Tavern
in the 1970s. Built ca. 1927 and housing two stores, the building is a classic example of
plantation-style, commercial vernacular architecture, with its false front and corrugated
metal roof. The building is not currently in use. *Florence Yonemoto Collection*

18

18 Yokouchi Bakery

The Yokouchi brothers take a break outside their Yokouchi Bakery ca. 1955. They are (*left to right*) Shigeo "Boss" Yokouchi, Noriaki "Spud" Yokouchi and Saburo "Nut" Yokouchi. A fourth brother, Masaru "Pundy" Yokouchi, also worked at the popular shop on the northeast corner of Church and Vineyard. The location still houses a bakery today — the Maui Bake Shop.

Sandy Yoshimori Collection

25 Main Street USA

By the 1930s Main Street sported a line-up of stores and services that typified small town America.
This parade moving west up Main passes the Bank of Hawaii, the U.S. Post Office, the Orpheum Theater, Home
Furnishings, the Maui Dry Goods & Grocery Liquor Dealer (**25**) and a rooming house. When the Orpheum — first
opened in 1901 — was rebuilt 20 years later, it offered movie buffs an alternative to Wailuku's only other movie house
at the time, the Hippodrome on Market Street. In 1966 the State of Hawai'i erected the office building that
stands today in the area on the right. *Maui Historical Society*

26 Home Furnishings

In 1913, Maui Dry Goods & Grocery Co. opened a department store on Main Street near the old livery stables. Boasting the largest plate glass windows in the Territory and selling a variety of products from food to furniture, the new emporium drew rubberneckers from all over the island. The building served as MDG&G's Wailuku branch until 1952, when it became Home Furnishings, offering a complete line of household goods. It is shown here in 1960, before it was torn down to make way for today's federal office building.
Wayne Tanaka Collection

22 First National Bank of Wailuku

In 1904 three-year-old First National — Maui's first banking institution — moved into this frame structure
on Main leased from the Church of the Good Shepherd. Reconstruction of the old parsonage revealed beams bearing
the initials GBW, for Good Shepherd founder Rev. George B. Whipple, who had built it in the 1860s. Described by
management as "one of the handsomest buildings in Wailuku" — and by other observers as "pretentious" —
it became the headquarters in 1917 for the new Bank of Maui. The building was razed in 1982. *Bank of Hawaii*

"It's Big and Bright and Strong!"

Everything comes to him who waits,
And we have waited long,
But never mind — look what we have!
And it's Big! and Bright! and Strong!

Come all you wise men, for what do we care
To whom the moneys belong?
And put them in a place you know
Is Big! and Bright! and Strong!

Don't let a fire destroy your Bonds,
Or an enemy do you wrong,
Just rest in peace, and leave them with us,
Where it's Big! and Bright! and Strong!

Did you ever see such a huge vault door?
Come on and join the throng,
And put your money where you know it's safe,
For it's Big! and Bright! and Strong!

Now where do you want your money kept?
This surely will be your song:
"I'll put it in the Maui Bank,
'Cause it's Big! and Bright! and Strong!"

— Lyrics by anonymous Bank of Maui employee, ca. 1920

27 Bank of Hawaii

Batons twirl and a brass band plays as a parade passes the Bank of Hawaii and adjoining Post Office
on its way down Main Street ca. 1940s. Built in 1919 as an expansion of the Bank of Maui, it opened with great
fanfare — "cigars and cigarettes for the men," the *Maui News* reported, "bonbons for the ladies" — and became the
Wailuku branch of Bank of Hawaii when the two institutions merged in 1930. The building was remodeled and
expanded from the 1950s through the '70s and is still a Bank of Hawaii branch today. *Maui Historical Society*

29 Maui Grand Hotel

The Maui Grand was considered the island's finest lodging in its heyday, after it opened with a gala "booster banquet" for the 1916 Maui County Fair. The posh hotel on Main lured such celebrity guests as Will Rogers, Bing Crosby, Cecil B. DeMille and Georgia O'Keeffe. When its swank new cocktail lounge opened to the sounds of Harry Owens and his Orchestrain 1935, it was billed as the first soundproof, air-conditioned lounge in the Territory. The building was razed in 1961, when Uptown Service Station was built on the site. *Wayne Tanaka Collection*

29 Molina's Orchestra

This popular combo played Saturday night dance music at the Maui Grand in the late 1940s. Organized around five brothers of the musical Molina family, of Keahua Camp near Pāʻia, the orchestra included (*left to right, front row*) Robert Oshiro, Domingo Molina, Sal Molina, Henry Molina and Tony Molina and, (*left to right, back*) Frank Flores, Akira Watanabe, Benito Martins, Joe Molina, Eddie Viloria and Edwin Lavilla. Molina's Orchestra also performed at military camps and high school dances all over Maui and Lānaʻi. *Domingo Molina Collection*

26

31 30 Maui Book Store and S.H. Kress & Co.

The Maui Book Store (**31**) opened on Main Street in 1923. Twelve years later the Kress store (**30**) — a popular Wailuku retail fixture — opened next door on land purchased from Wailuku Sugar Co., under the storefront sign that read, S.H. Kress & Co. 5-10-25 Cent Store. The crowds who flocked to Wailuku from all over Maui for Kress' grand opening found state-of-the-art commercial design and the trademark Kress candy counter. The store was expanded in 1948. Today the remodeled Kress building provides office space for Wailuku professionals. *Doris Hotta Collection*

In 1951 Koyoshi Kato bought the Maui Book Store building next to the New York Dress Shop (*at left*) and moved her 17-year-old dry goods business to Wailuku from its original home in Kahului. Kato Dry Goods is shown here at its grand opening, on August 14, 1951. After her store closed in 1982, the building held a succession of eateries. Today the neatly renovated space houses Cafe O'lei at 2051 Main Street. *Elaine Kato Tamasaka Collection*

27

28

33 Valley Isle Motors

In 1925 Valley Isle Motors expanded its Ford Motors sales and service operation into this spacious showroom on Main between Market and Church, shown here in 1960 across from the National Dollar Store. Today the former dealership is being redeveloped as part of the Main Street Promenade, a major commercial complex to include retail shops and a food court. *Wayne Tanaka Collection*

34 Wailuku Hardware & Grocery
Shown here in the 1920s, Wailuku Hardware & Grocery had opened in 1914 and moved to the northwest corner of Main and Market three years later. A meat market and a new exterior were added in 1927. When Wailuku Hardware closed in 1937, it was replaced by the Main Market, billed as a modern shopping center, with concessions including a meat market, four fish markets, the Tarashita Pickle Counter and Lau Fresh Pork, Roast Pork, Duck & Chicken. Before Wailuku Hardware, a theater showing silent movies stood at this spot. *Maui Historical Society*

30

35 Market and Main

A silver Kahului Railroad Co. bus headed for Pāʻia stops ca. 1938 in front of the kindergarten of the Alexander House Settlement, a community center opened at the turn of the century on the southwest corner of Main and Market. This center also housed the Chamber of Commerce, Red Cross and Community Chest. The Maui Book Store and S.H. Kress are visible further up the street while directly across Main, Wailuku Hardware & Grocery has been replaced by the Main Market. *Roy Crabb/Hawaiʻi State Archives*

35 National Dollar Store

In this 1960 photo taken from the same spot, the Main Market has given way to Mike's Department Store, while the Alexander House Settlement kindergarten has been replaced by National Dollar Stores' Wailuku outlet. This was National Dollar Co.'s third Hawai'i location, built on a parcel purchased from Wailuku Sugar Co. in 1950. Today, the restored National Dollar building is the home of the Maui Academy of Performing Arts. *Wayne Tanaka Collection*

41 **40** Maui Dry Goods & Grocery

Early in the 20th Century a Japanese hospital stood at the southeast corner of Main and Market (**40**).
In 1937 Maui Dry Goods & Grocery completed this two-story structure on the site, housing its headquarters, the
Canton Chinese Restaurant and the Wailuku office of Theo H. Davies & Co. MDG&G opened its Liquor Department at
the corner of the building, shown here ca. 1940. At far left is MDG&G Co.'s Maui Book Store and Photo Studio (**41**),
built in 1932 as the Tanioka Photo Studio, where an independent book store operates today. *Maui Historical Society*

42 MDG&G Automotive Division

A parade ca. 1930 passes Maui Dry Goods & Grocery Co.'s Automotive Division, built in 1924
on two former Kalua Homestead Tract lots at Main and Maluhia Drive. The imposing structure housed a
showroom for General Motors automobiles. Today the Auto Division building and the Hanada Service Station
beyond are being redeveloped as the Dragon, a mixed-use commercial complex
to include offices, shops and a cafe. *Maui Historical Society*

43 Hanada Service Station

After servicing central Maui's motor trade at two different locations on Market Street, Yuichi Hanada opened his last and largest service station in the mid-'20s on Main and Maluhia. Hanada also built the adjoining home at the rear of the station to accommodate a growing family that included five girls and six boys — four of whom ran the station until it closed in 1980. A modern service station replaced this one in 1967 and today is being redeveloped as part of a new office and retail complex.

Yoshie Sato Collection

44 von Hamm-Young Company

In the late 1920s a Buddhist funeral procession forms up on Main in front of von Hamm-Young Co.'s service station (*far left*) and auto dealership (*opposite*). The Honolulu company opened its Maui used car operation in 1912, moving to Main Street in 1919. The gas station was added in 1924. The accessories store between the main showroom and the gas station opened in 1927 and offered, according to the *Maui News*, "magnetos, snubbers, horns,

side shields...everything from feather dusters to a new engine." Further up the street are the company's Dodge Brothers dealership and a turn-of-the-century building that once housed a Japanese hospital and was razed in 1936 to make way for Maui Dry Goods & Grocery's headquarters (*far right*). The funeral was probably held at the Wailuku Hongwanji Temple, just around the corner at Market and Wells. Today this area is the site of several office buildings between 1935 Main and the southwest corner of Market and Main. *Doris Hotta Collection*

"Wailuku Has Last Word in Service Station"

Up to the minute, as fine and complete as anything of the kind in Honolulu even if not so large as some of them, is the new service and filling station of von Hamm Young (*preceding pages*)... Situated just mauka of the Wailuku depot...it is so arranged that two cars headed in each direction, four at one time, can be served.

At the makai side and to the rear is a feature worthy of special comment, the raised runway where mechanics can go right under the car for oiling and greasing and changing the oil in motors. This obviates the necessity of the man working on the car lying down beneath it, assures a better job, and the patron can see, at the same time, just what is being done...

Evening service until 10 o'clock is furnished so that persons who are unable to bring their cars for attention in the daytime can do so in the evening. It is possible to leave the car, go to the theater or elsewhere and find it all ready for use when such engagements are ended.

Between the main establishment and the service station is the used car salesroom, completed even more recently than the service station... Such a room has the advantage of exhibiting used cars only in contrast with other used cars and not opening a comparison between used cars and new ones, which often discourages the prospective buyer of a used one.

With the three buildings on the street and the workshops and store houses at the back, the von Hamm Young Company is now occupying and utilizing a large area.

— *Maui News, April 11, 1924*

47 46 Shell Service Station
The modern era arrived in Wailuku here in 1953 with activation of Maui's first stoplight at Main and Central. Today, Maui Dry Goods & Grocery's long-standing Shell Station (**47**) has been replaced with a convenience store and other shops, while the Maui Realty Suites office building stands where the Chevron station and the Hymie J. Meyer Co. (**46**) appear across the street. Meyer had leased the old Wailuku Depot parcel in 1939.
Wayne Tanaka Collection

39

48 First Hanada Service Station

In the 1920s, Wailuku motorists enjoyed curbside service at Yuichi Hanada's station on the east side of Market, directly across from Baldwin Bank. Hanada also filled the tanks of his taxi and car rental fleet here. Among the automotive offerings: Red Crown gasoline and Zerolene motor oil. The portable compressor and tank in the doorway at left was used for servicing tires. Next door is the Wailuku Vulcanizing Works — telephone 147 — and beyond that, the dental offices of Dr. L.C. Smith (*far right*). *Yoshie Sato Collection*

49 **Bishop First National Bank**

In this view looking north along Market from Main ca. 1940, the stately concrete edifice of Bishop First National (*left center*) — which moved here in 1924 as Baldwin Bank — stands out among the less formal storefronts of its neighbors. For years the bank shared the space with Maui Electric Co. In 1933 Baldwin Bank became Bishop First National Bank, which built a new steel-frame structure here in 1964. Five years after that, Bishop First National became First Hawaiian Bank, whose Wailuku branch still occupies the location today. *George Emura Collection*

49 Maui Electric Company

Management and staff pose outside MECO's Market Street office in 1926, five years after the utility was formed to provide reliable electric service to Wailuku and Kahului. Beginning with some 500 residential and commercial customers, MECO soon extended this service to the ranching and agricultural communities of Pāʻia, Haʻikū, Kula and Makawao. The utility shared the building with Baldwin Bank, later Bishop First National Bank. The Wailuku branch of First Hawaiian Bank is located here today. *Hawaiian Electric Co.*

44

50 33 North Market Street
Wailuku's 1953 Christmas Parade rolls down Market past Maui Drugs, Herbert's Furniture,
the Maui Standard Market with its rooming house upstairs, and Ted's Men's Wear, in the buildings
just to the north of today's First Hawaiian Bank. This Market Street frontage is now the site
of the 33 Market Street office building. *Wayne Tanaka Collection*

51 46 N. Market Street

At the sign of the muscleman, Olympic weightlifter and bodybuilding consultant Tommy Kono operated his Maui Health Center, shown here in 1964, on the east side of Market between Main and Vineyard. Kono shared the building with Maui Sportswear, Clyde's Shoes and Palms Travel. Several of the street's early 20th-Century frame buildings survive today including the one just visible at right, which in 1964 housed Johnny's Sportswear, a pool room and the Mabuhay Barber Shop. *Aluli Trust Estate*

46

52 Maui Savings & Loan

In 1962 Maui Savings & Loan (*center*) opened on Market, in a building which also housed Shiyan Okazu-ya.
In 1970, this structure and the former Chinese restaurant building at Pili Street (*right*) made way for today's American
Savings & Loan branch. Viewed to the left of Maui Savings here are Makino Shoe Store in the Goodness Building,
currently an empty lot; Nakagawa Tailor, now the site of Sig Zane Design; and Emura Jewelry, still doing business
at this location today after more than a half-century on Market Street.

American Savings & Loan

53 Hanada Auto Stand

Former plantation worker Yuichi Hanada (*far right*) started this taxi stand and car rental business ca. 1910. A blacksmith shared the space at Hanada Auto Stand, whose drivers traveled in their Model-T Fords and a Hudson Essex (*right*) as far afield as Lahaina. Hanada, his wife and the first of his 11 children lived upstairs. The stand was located just off Market on the north side of Kalua Avenue, later renamed Pili Street. Today, this section of Pili Street has been covered over by Wailuku's municipal parking lot. *Yoshie Sato Collection*

"Ill-fated trio swept into the sea..."

After four days of weary and dangerous searching of the angry waters off Kahakuloa, the badly battered remains of Harold Fujimoto and the partial remains of Gilbert Hotta have been recovered by rescuers... The body of (Dr. Hideo Tamura), the third member of Monday night's tragedy has not been found. The remains of Mr. Fujimoto were recovered about 100 yards from where the ill-fated trio was swept into the sea... Enough of the remains of Mr. Hotta were recovered from a huge shark caught on Thursday...for identification.

— *Maui News, January 8, 1950*

The three of them were fishing from the cliffs at Kahakuloa that night, when these big waves came in about ten o'clock and swept them off the rocks. After the alert was sounded by Harold's brother Wayman, who was the only survivor, it seemed like the whole island was out there looking for them — police divers and all. They had seen several sharks in the area and a sampan just happened to catch this one. When they opened it up, there was my husband — although they still had to identify him with dental records and fingerprints. They never did find Dr. Tamura.

Keeping the store going was hard, since we had four small children at the time. I didn't know anything about business, and it was unusual in those days for a woman to do something like that. But everybody knew our story and would come in to support the store. Slowly we built it up and pretty soon we were supplying jackets for just about every prom in the county! Also weddings, luaus, grad parties — you name it.

I felt I owed it to my husband. After all, he had only opened for business one month before the accident.

— *Susanne Hotta, proprietor, Gilbert's Formal Wear*

51 Gilbert's Formal Wear

Hotta family members and friends, including owners Susanne Hotta (*left*) and Gilbert Hotta (*right*) pose at the December 1949 grand opening of their tuxedo shop. The Market and Vineyard corner location had previously been Frankie and Johnnie's lunch counter. At right center, wearing glasses, is Gilbert's mother, Shina Hotta, who had opened Hotta Store nearly a half-century before (*page 53*). One month after this photo was taken, Gilbert Hotta drowned in a fishing accident. Susanne Hotta carried on, creating a small business success story that continues today.

Susanne Hotta Collection

54 Harry's Sweets

A 40-year fixture at the Iao Theatre, Harry Kaya ran the snack concession there from the mid-1930s through the mid-'70s. With his trademark cigar and his dog Queenie, the former Wailuku Sugar chemist was a theater popcorn pioneer on Maui. Harry's Sweets was located outside the theater entrance on Market Street. The 700-seat Iao Theater, which opened in 1928 with the silent film "Sporting Goods," was named not after 'Iao Valley but for the *iao*, a small bait fish popular with Maui anglers. Today the building is the home of the Maui Community Theatre.
George Kaya Collection

58 Molina's Bar

The Market Street watering hole that became a Wailuku institution appears shortly after it opened in 1960 in a building that once housed a fish market. Two years later owner Manuel Molina helped launch the Wailuku Federal Credit Union and later held public office for more than 20 years. In 1962 he added the Mountain View Rooms behind his bar, using some of the fixtures and materials from the recently demolished Maui Grand Hotel. Under new ownership today, it is named the Manuel S. Molina Sports Bar & Rooms in honor of its colorful founder. *Wayne Tanaka Collection*

57 Old Wailuku fish market

Photographed ca. 1910, this fish market on the southeast corner of Market and Mill
was an open-air establishment with cast iron pillars supporting a corrugated metal roof. The stone steps
and angled retaining wall remain today. Previous use of this parcel included a plantation house
where Mark Twain, while on assignment with the *Sacramento Union* in 1866, stayed for five weeks
with a Wailuku Sugar Co. supervisor. *Maui Historical Society*

56 **Hotta Store**
Bunkichi Hotta (*left*), his wife Shina and toddler Ted pose with a barber (*holding carriage*) from a nearby shop ca. 1907. The Japanese characters assure affordable prices, while the Hawaiian sign translates as "house to buy clothing." This store was later the site of Yoda Fish Market. The renovated Miranda Building still exists today as the 140 North Market Building — complete with the iron rings in the sidewalk once used by local riders to tether their horses.
Doris Hotta Collection

56 North Market Street

Buildings on the east side of Market near Mill appear ca. 1930s behind the angled retaining wall still there today. They include (*left to right*) a wood-frame Chinese store, today the site of an antique store and other shops; the F.M. Pires Building, which housed the Pires family meat market and is still standing today; and the Miranda Building, which then housed Yoda Fish Market. As indicated by the Salvation Army sign silhouetted at right, that organization's headquarters were located just across from the Chinese store. *Yukioshi Yoda Collection*

56 Yoda Fish Market

The Yoda brothers started their fish market in the F.M. Pires Building then expanded into this grocery store
next door in the Miranda Building, where they lived upstairs with their families. The brothers bought fresh fish
from fishermen in Kahului, Ma'alaea and Kīhei, while their wives and children helped around the store — splitting
wood for the stove, or raising chickens and rabbits in the back yard. Several of the Yoda children also worked after
school for Wailuku Sugar Co., cutting grass or hoeing the fields for 50 cents a day. *Yukioshi Yoda Collection*

60 Happy Valley Flood
The lower north end of Market Street looks much the same today as it did in December 1950,
when torrential rains triggered a flood that drowned a teenage boy who was washed away in a car, destroyed
a bridge, and caused extensive damage to shops and homes. Floodwaters from overflowing ʻĪao Stream rose to
the dark spot in the white paint on the telephone pole at right center. The disaster prompted a public outcry
that resulted in some major flood control projects. *Wailuku Agribusiness*

61 **Takamiya Store**
Still a fixture in Happy Valley today, this classic Wailuku mom-and-pop store is located
on the west side of Market Street. Here founder Kenneth Takamiya stands by his grocery delivery
truck in 1947, a year after the store opened for business. Takamiya lived on the second floor
with his wife and family. *Kenneth Takamiya Collection*

68 **Aloha Lodge**

In 1901 the Maui chapter of the Knights of Pythias fraternal organization began construction of their Aloha Lodge Building, a two-story structure near Mill Street and Lower Main that would house the lodge upstairs and rental space downstairs. As a 1913 community service project, Lodge membership sponsored a new park at the nearby corner of Mill and Main. By 1919 this building had been vacated.

Maui Historical Society

68 Knights of Pythias

Dog and boy join Lodge members posing on the building's front steps. The Ah Kee Saloon occupies most of the ground floor, no doubt enhancing the building's desirability as a meeting venue. A sign over the open doorway on the right identifies it as the entrance to the Aloha Lodge meeting area upstairs. *Maui Historical Society*

"Don't worry about it. The horse will know where to go."

My grandfather, Manuel Nobriga, started working here in 1922. His first day on the job, he was given a horsecart and told to make the daily ice deliveries around town. When he asked about the route, they told him, "Don't worry about it. The horse will know where to go."

So he got in the cart with the ice and the tongs, and right away the horse headed out for the first house on the route. When they got there, my grandfather climbed down, picked up a block of ice with the tongs and took it in to the icebox. When he came back, he threw the tongs in the back of the cart. As soon as the horse heard that, he took off for the next stop, with my grandfather standing there watching him go! He ran after the cart and finally caught up with it at the next house where he delivered the ice. Then, of course, the horse took off again. My grandfather said he chased that cart all over town that day and the horse knew right where to stop every time!

That was the start of our family's history with Maui Soda. Later my grandfather was assistant manager, then manager, then part of a new ownership group. He managed the company for 33 years and worked here almost 50 years total. My father and uncle also worked here, and today there are six of us grandchildren involved in the day-to-day operations.

— *Catherine Nobriga Kim, Ice Cream Manager, Maui Soda & Ice Works*

🔳70 Maui Soda & Ice Works

One of Wailuku's longest-running companies is Maui Soda & Ice, located on Lower Main Street since the
turn of the century. Ralph Wadsworth and his son David, who had owned the company since 1899, operated out
of their home and adjoining warehouse, shown here ca. 1910. The company provided horsecart service to homes and
commercial establishments as far afield as Kīhei and Haʻikū, dispensing blocks of ice along with soda water, ginger ale,
root beer, strawberry soda, fruit syrups and a celery and iron concoction. *Maui Historical Society*

70 Maui Soda & Ice Works

By the late '20s the horsecarts had given way to a large fleet of trucks with a full complement of drivers. After David Wadsworth's death the distribution company was managed by his sister Frances through World War II. The company was later acquired by a group of workers and investors — including long-time employee Manuel Nobriga — and is today a Nobriga family-owned business with more than 65 employees and some $12 million in annual revenues.

Maui Soda & Ice Works

3 Wailuku Union Church

Photographed ca. 1915 not long after its completion, the Gothic-style structure on High Street appears without any of the tropical foliage and tall trees that surround it today. Built of stone gathered from Wailuku Sugar Co. fields and 'Iao Valley, the church was erected around a cornerstone laid in 1911. The cross atop the gable at left was carved from a single stone. The new edifice replaced a small frame church built in 1867 at the current site of the old County Office Building (**6**) across High Street.

Wailuku Union Church

64

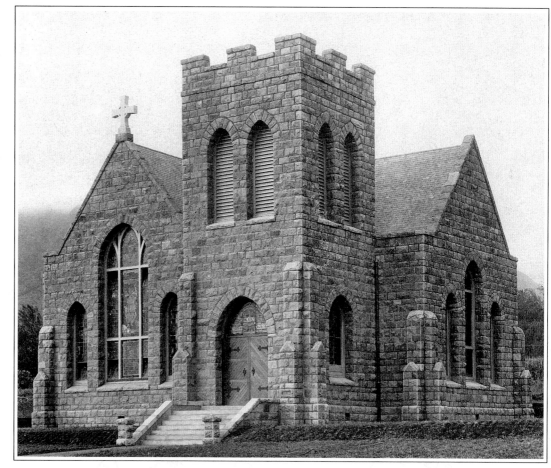

CHAPTER THREE
The Churches of Wailuku

🔵5 🔵9 Ka'ahumanu Church

In 1908 the old Wailuku Courthouse was moved across the street onto the church-leased corner parcel at left, first as the Wailuku Town Hall and, after that, the Little Theater community playhouse. It made way in 1930 for the C.W. Dickey-designed Territorial Building — now a State office building (**5**) — that stands there today. By the time of this photo ca. 1905, Ka'ahumanu Church had been serving the Hawaiian community for 70 years — originally a thatched structure built over the former *heiau* of 18th-Century chief Kahekili. The Maui Hotel appears at right. *Bishop Museum*

◆9 Ka'ahumanu Church

Today's church, the fourth to be built on the site, was designed in the classic New England tradition by Wailuku Sugar Co. manager Edward Bailey in honor of Ka'ahumanu, the powerful queen who helped establish Christianity in the Islands. Here in early 1903, Hawaiian women prepare a *lū'au* on the church grounds. Featuring kālua pig, fish and poi, the feast was held for the children of the Alexander House Settlement kindergarten, who marched together through town for a few hours of games and good eating. *Kitty Gay Burkland Collection/Hawai'i State Archives*

⑭ Iao Congregational Church

Opened in 1936 as Wailuku Japanese Christian, this graceful structure became Iao Congregational soon after the outbreak of World War II. The church is shown here during the war, when military restrictions dictated that meetings could only be held by day and that withdrawal of church funds were subject to government review. Iao Congregational hired its first full-time English-speaking minister in 1946 and today hosts a diverse, multi-ethnic congregation.

Iao Congregational Church

🔹 Wailuku Japanese Christian Church

Wailuku's non-Buddhist Japanese residents built this church and social hall on the southeast corner of Church and Vineyard in 1909. They had long since outgrown their previous facility, which was a Wailuku Sugar Co. plantation house that the church purchased and moved to the corner of Mill and Market in 1896 — when the congregation consisted of just 12 Japanese immigrants. Here in the early 1930s, the top of the Gee Kung Tong Society house (**17**) can be seen at right center. *Iao Congregational Church*

Church members gather ca. 1930 on the steps of the social hall on Church Street. In 1936 Wailuku Japanese Christian was moved further up Vineyard, where the historic Kanda Home (*pages 90-92*) was relocated on the grounds to make way for the new facility. Wailuku Japanese Christian was renamed Iao Congregational Church during World War II.

Iao Congregational Church

71

72

Christmas afternoon was devoted to preparing the tree for the Sunday-school children. They number in all about fifty: of these fifteen are white children, and the rest are half-caste and Hawaiian. There is one little Chinese girl among them. Some of them had never seen a Christmas tree, and we were glad to furnish one...

My young readers, who have been accustomed to beautiful fir and cedar trees, will smile when I tell them how our tree was made. We stripped the large leaves from a kind of tree that grows here, and wound its branches with leaves of...a beautiful trailing evergreen, which the natives call "wa-wae-i-o-le," meaning mouse-foot... this, with another vine, which the natives are very fond of, on account of the sweet smell of its smooth, shining green leaves, is what was used for trimming the Chapel. Some of the "greens" were gathered on the sides of the high mountains near here, and some were brought twenty-five miles by some Hawaiian boys, who took great delight in gathering them, and in helping to put them up afterwards...

But it was a very pretty tree after all when it was finished and hung with its gay little candy bags — you see we have candy away off here — its bright dolls and scarfs, its boxes and books, and balls, and tops, and pictures: and it was prettier still when it was lighted up... with its many little candles.

The happy time...was at length over, and...the children sang "Wonderful Night," and went home, happy with their prizes, and I hope, to be happy many times in the recollection of this first Christmas in Wailuku.

Yours very truly,
Mary J. Whipple

— Letter to friends in New England from the wife of Rev. George Whipple, Church of the Good Shepherd

⟐ Church of the Good Shepherd Parsonage
In 1866 Rev. George Whipple and his congregation built the original
Church of the Good Shepherd (*left*) at Main and Church, where Wailuku's first English language church
services were held. Here it is used as a school and parish hall, having been moved back in 1910 to make
way for a new church. The parsonage at right was added in about 1903 and stands approximately
at the site of today's 55 N. Church office building. *Church of the Good Shepherd*

🔲 **Church of the Good Shepherd**
Congregation members gather in 1910 for the laying of the cornerstone for a new
Good Shepherd Church at the northwest corner of Main and Church. The cornerstone appears at left center,
a few feet to the right of Mrs. L.M. Baldwin, who provides musical accompaniment on the organ. The new church
was consecrated on Easter Sunday 1911 and appears today, with additions and renovations,
much as it did then. *Church of the Good Shepherd*

39 Wailuku Hongwanji Mission

Maui's first Jodo Shinshu Buddhist minister, Rev. Hojun Kunisaki, arrived on the island in 1898, setting up shop in a small shack behind what is now First Hawaiian Bank on Market. In 1902 the new Wailuku Hongwanji Mission completed its first temple, seen here at the corner of Wells and Market.

Wailuku Hongwanji Mission

🔟 Wailuku Hongwanji Mission

In 1918 Wailuku Hongwanji bought an adjoining lot at Wells and Market and added a student dormitory and minister's residence. Here the congregation gathers just after the opening of the new facility. The mission was idled during the war years, when the military built an air raid shelter on the site. Today this is the location of the Valley Isle Marine Center. *Wailuku Hongwanji Mission*

✦ YBA Hall

In 1937 the Young Buddhist Association added this social hall to its Japanese Language School on Vineyard and Kaniela. Both hall and school were closed during the war, then reopened in 1945 when Wailuku Hongwanji Mission relocated there from Market and Wells, using the YBA Hall as its place of worship. At Wailuku Hongwanji's centennial in 1988, the entire complex was renovated as the temple that exists today. *Wailuku Hongwanji Mission*

14 Roman Catholic Cemetery

Marianist priests tend the church cemetery in 1895. The Marianists had arrived on Maui in 1883, ten years after the opening of St. Anthony's Church (*background*). Among other distinctions, the church was where Father Damien de Veuster first volunteered to work with residents of the Hansen's disease colony on the island of Moloka'i. The Marianists continue to guide both the church and St. Anthony Schools today. *Brother Bertram Photo/Maui Historical Society*

✠ Mass at St. Anthony's

Parishioners attend Mass shortly after the crucifix was added in 1942. In November 1977 the historic church was destroyed by a fire set by an arsonist — an inferno which completely gutted the structure and destroyed priceless stained glass windows, both organs, an 1858 bell and the altar pictured here. The church was built anew and reopened as St. Anthony's Church Center in June 1980. *St. Anthony's Church*

❷ Wailuku Elementary School

Mrs. Cecilia Soule's fourth-grade class poses on the school's north side steps in 1960.
Built in 1904 with stone gathered from ʻĪao Valley and Wailuku Sugar Co. land, the handsome structure
replaced a ramshackle public facility previously in use at the corner of High and Kaohu. First called Wailuku
Public School, it was renamed Wailuku Elementary in 1928 with the debut of nearby Iao School,
which was then known as Wailuku Junior High School. *Yuki Lei Sugimura Collection*

CHAPTER FOUR
School Days

"The handsomest school building on the island..."

In 1904, a prominent Honolulu architect described the new building as "the handsomest school building on the island or perhaps the country." The stones...were of equal grade to (Honolulu's) Kamehameha Chapel and even better quality than the stone used on Central Union Church on Oahu.

All that praise and attention was directed toward the new Wailuku Public School, built on what used to be a cow pasture just down the road from a deteriorating wooden school house. The old school was operating on the premises of the Wailuku Union Church on the corner of High Street and Kaohu Street. It was considered an eyesore and a health hazard. Editorials in the Maui News deplored the conditions of the building, calling it "immoral and unsanitary," and advocated its removal. At the same time, editorials encouraged the construction of a brick building which would be a lasting monument and pride for the community.

On May 23, 1904, the building was dedicated with school children coming by train to attend the ceremony. The Wailuku Brass Band played Hawaii Ponoi, and Charles King the laureate musician of the Territory performed. The Superintendent of Public Instruction, A.T. Atkinson, spoke of the history of the chief's schools, the mission and private schools, and the evolution of public schools. He spoke of how Hawaiians could not marry until they could read and write. He spoke of how adults went to school along with children because they too needed an education. And at one time there were 25 common schools and 7 Catholic schools in Wailuku alone. And of the 900 schools in the Territory at the beginning of the century, the new Wailuku Public School was the crown jewel of them all.

Then Senator H.P. Baldwin laid the cornerstone and buried a steel tube containing an 1866 copy of the Hawaiian Gazette; a 1904 copy of the Maui News; some American and Hawaiian coins; Hawaiian stamps; reports from the Hawaiian Commercial & Sugar Co.; a 1903 government report; and the constitution of the School Improvement Association.

A year later... students planted the Royal palms as an Arbor Day project...lining the semi-circular driveway.

— D. Sonny Gamponia
A Brief History of Wailuku Elementary School

❷ Wailuku Elementary School

Students ca. 1950s hit the books in a classroom still in use today. During World War II, classes were held in Wailuku churches and community buildings, when the U.S. Army commandeered the school as a headquarters and barracks. Most of the concrete block classrooms adjoining the original building were added in 1951. *Wailuku Elementary School*

38 37 Alexander House Settlement

This 11-acre community center was named in honor of early Wailuku missionaries William and Mary Alexander. The settlement originally encompassed a Chinese church (**37**) (*right*) on Market Street and a kindergarten on the corner of Market and Main. Young women who taught at the kindergarten roomed at a boarding house (**38**) (*left*) further along Market. In this 1902 photograph, Wells Street has yet to be built just past the church, and Market Street is still a year away from being paved.

Kitty Gay Burkland Collection/ Hawai'i State Archives

The teachers' rooming house offered private and semi-private rooms for the school's young single teachers, each including a small desk and other homey furnishings. Photographer Kitty Gay — one of the Settlement's first teachers — labeled this 1902 photo of the house "Old Maids' Paradise."

Kitty Gay Burkland Collection/Hawai'i State Archives

85

36 Alexander House Settlement Kindergarten
Schoolchildren pose in the Settlement yard ca. 1905. Later, instruction at the Settlement for older children included sewing classes, mechanical drawing, and English classes for Chinese and Japanese immigrants.
Maui Historical Society

35 Alexander House Settlement

In 1924 the original kindergarten was demolished and two new buildings, designed in Spanish
Mission style, were added to the southwest frontages of Main and Market. The expanded facility offered
learning space for "80 bright little kiddies," the *Maui News* reported. Here students stand on the steps
of the Settlement's brand new kindergarten, as the Valley Isle Motors showroom
nears completion across Main Street. *Maui Historical Society*

36 35 Alexander House Settlement

The new Settlement office building (**36**) (*opposite*) and school (**35**) appear in the mid-1920s at Market and Main. A gymnasium, swimming pool and bowling alley were added in 1911 and later, a library and other athletic facilities. The Settlement hosted concerts, parties and Scouting activities and ran community outreach programs in health care and physical education. After the Settlement closed in 1950, the structures were replaced by National Dollar Store and American Security Bank. Today the corner bank site is being redeveloped as an office building.
Maui Historical Society

15 Kanda Home

In July 1914 Shigefusa and Sue Kanda opened their beautiful new Kanda Home for Girls on a large parcel between Main and Vineyard. The Kandas had launched the school in 1911 in their own home at Main and Market, boarding and educating young Japanese girls from many of Maui's outlying areas. The building was relocated on the Vineyard property in 1936, when a new Wailuku Japanese Christian Church — later renamed Iao Congregational Church — was built on the site.

Iao Congregational Church

90

15 Kanda Home

Shigefusa Kanda (*back row, center*) poses with associates on the lawn of the Kanda Home at its grand opening celebration in 1914. Nineteen years earlier, the Christian missionary had emigrated from Japan to the Big Island of Hawai'i, where he built a church, established Hawaii's first Japanese language school and championed the rights of Japanese plantation laborers. In 1906 he moved his family to Maui, where he sold insurance and launched a short-lived newspaper before helping his wife manage the Kanda Home. *Iao Congregational Church*

92

🄸 Kanda Home

Approximately 75 girls lived at the Kanda Home, attending public school in the mornings and receiving further instruction in the Japanese arts and Christian values from Sue Kanda and her staff in the afternoons and evenings. Here students practice the violin and *koto* ca. 1915 on a tatami mat floor. Girls also received intensive training in Japanese language, calligraphy, flower arranging, etiquette and tea ceremony. The building was demolished in 1953 to make way for the Iao Congregational parking lot.

Iao Congregational Church

66 **St. Anthony Boys School**

Students stand by their schoolhouse at St. Anthony in the early 1900s. The school was opened by three Marianist priests in September 1883, with 62 students comprising three classes in a single room. By the end of the first term, the physical plant had been expanded and enrollment had risen to 105. Tuition at St. Anthony at the time was 38 cents per month.

Brother Bertram Photo/Maui Historical Society

67 St. Anthony Girls School

In January 1884, a small group of Franciscan nuns established the girl's school and nearby Malulani Hospital at the request of Queen Kapi'olani. The school's first principal was Sister Mary Antonella, who died in 1885 — the result of an illness she contracted on the boat from Honolulu to Maui. She is buried in the Catholic cemetery adjacent to the St. Anthony Church and School complex. The Franciscans guided St. Anthony Girls School until 1928, when a group of Maryknoll sisters arrived to manage the facility.

Brother Bertram Photo/St. Anthony School

🔢 St. Anthony School Faculty
Flanked by carefully placed potted plants, these no-nonsense instructors pose at
the school sometime between 1921 and 1924. Left to right: Brother James Murphy, Brother
Raymond McGonagle, Brother William Schuetz, Brother Leo Schaeffer
and Brother Nicholas Waldeck. *St. Anthony School*

4 **Maui County Free Library**

In 1919 the Maui Women's Club started the island's first public library in the former Robinson home
on High Street. This Maui County Free Library is shown here in 1928, a year before today's Wailuku Public Library,
designed by Honolulu's C.W. Dickey, opened on the corner parcel at High and Kaohu Streets.
In 1878 the large monkeypod tree at left shaded the island's first public telephone.

Maui Historical Society

CHAPTER FIVE
Small Town Services

8 Wailuku Courthouse

As the 19th Century drew to a close, Wailuku's judiciary was hearing cases in a small, shabby courthouse on High Street. So limited was this facility that the grand jury was often forced to meet elsewhere—in a church basement, an old schoolhouse or the basement of the jail. The old courthouse, built ca. 1880 and photographed here sometime between 1897 and 1901, was moved across the street in 1908 to become the Wailuku Town Hall.

Frank Davey/Bishop Museum

⚠8 Wailuku Courthouse
Shriners gather on the steps of Circuit Court ca. 1917 in the midst of a mass initiation. Built in 1907, two years after Wailuku was named the seat of government for the newly formed Maui County, the new courthouse was designed in the Beaux Arts Revival style. Now serving as office space for the County prosecutor, it sports a clay tile hip roof added in the '20s to complement a new County Office Building (**6**) built a half-block to the west on High Street.
Maui Historical Society

Photo by
T. Okumura.

Luau given by the Hawaiian
of Tandy Mackenzie at W...

⑧ ⑦ ⑥ Old Fire Station and Jail
Internationally acclaimed Tandy Mackenzie, a Hāna native, returned to Maui in 1922 for concerts
of operatic, secular and Hawaiian music in Wailuku and Kahului. Known as the "Hawaiian Caruso," Mackenzie poses
with guests on the lawn of the Wailuku Town Hall (**5**) on High Street, where he was the featured attraction at a *lu'au*
hosted by the Hawaiian Ladies Society. Visible across the street are the Wailuku Courthouse (**8**) (*behind tree, center*) and

Society in honor
Hall July 4

the County Jail and Fire Station (**7**), completed in 1907. Today the jail site is the location of the nine-story County Office Building, Wailuku's tallest structure. Two years after this photograph was taken, construction would begin just to the right of the jail on the first County Office Building (**6**). Still standing today, this Mediterranean-style building houses the County of Maui Planning Department.

Peris Collection/Maui Historical Society

⚠ Gee Kung Tong Society

Not a public building but a gathering place for single Chinese men, this was one of six of Maui's Gee Kung Tong society buildings, this one serving Wailuku and central Maui. Opened and dedicated in January 1905, it offered Chinese immigrants a place to visit, play *pai gow* or stay the night while traveling. The ornate but dilapidated structure, photographed here in the early 1990s, finally collapsed early one morning in 1995. All that remains today are the foundation and a concrete entry gate inscribed with Chinese characters. *County of Maui*

69 Malulani Hospital

Named Malulani — "under the protection of heaven" — by Queen Kapiʻolani after a visit, this medical facility was founded along with St. Anthony Girls School by Franciscan nuns in 1884. The structure was in use until the 1920s. The building that replaced it became the Hale Makua long-term care facility in 1953, a year after Maui Memorial Hospital opened between Wailuku and Kahului. The current Hale Makua facility was built on this site in 1966. *Maui Historical Society*

45 County Fairgrounds

Maui's first County Fair was held in 1916 at the Wells Park baseball field, in the area now occupied by an extension of Wells Street and the current park. This colorful event, which netted $2,000 over $5,000 in expenses, included a children's parade, a tractor exhibit, the Honolulu Zoo elephant Daisy, and a procession featuring half of the automobiles then operating on the island. Governor Lucius Pinkham delivered the opening address, urging island residents to prepare for war on a global scale. Subsequent Maui County Fairs were staged at the Kahului Fairgrounds. *Maui Historical Society*

46 Wailuku Depot

In 1879 Kahului Railroad began hauling milled sugar from Wailuku to Kahului Harbor. Eventually the line served plantation towns as far east as Kuiaha. Regular commuters included central Maui students attending Maui High School, which opened in 1913 at Hāmākuapoko. Though Kahului Railroad Co. replaced its passenger service with public bus service in 1935, its trains carried freight until 1966. The Maui Realty Suites office building stands at the Wailuku Depot site today. *Marvin Severson/Bird of Paradise Antiques*

⭐ Lufkin Residence

Banker C.D. Lufkin, who organized both First National Bank of Wailuku and the Bank of Maui, built this Craftsman-style home as a wedding gift for his son and daughter-in-law in 1924. One of the real showplaces of old Wailuku, the home has been meticulously restored to its original shine as The Old Wailuku Inn at Ulupono, a popular bed-and-breakfast. The Inn's seven guest rooms reflect the genteel ambience of Hawai'i in the 1920s and '30s. *Lucia Lufkin Mounts Collection*

CHAPTER SIX
Home Sweet Wailuku

✪ Alexander Mission Home

In 1902 lush foliage covered much of this National Historic Site built in 1837 and named for late-
19th-Century Wailuku Parish minister William Alexander. (William's daughter Emily later founded the Alexander
House Settlement on Main and Market in honor of her parents.) In 1919 the Alexander Mission Home was deeded to
the Maui Aid Association as a parsonage for the ministers of Wailuku Union Church, which it remains today.

Kitty Gay Burkland Collection/Hawai'i State Archives

⭐️13 Wailuku Sugar Manager's Residence

Built by Wailuku Sugar Co. for its managers, this building, photographed ca. 1900, was razed in 1937,
a year after a new manager's residence was built nearby. That building — today a private home adjacent to the
Maui Historical Society's Bailey House Museum — was designed by famed Honolulu architect C.W. Dickey
to serve as social and administrative headquarters for Wailuku Sugar.

Maui Historical Society

⭐12 Bailey House

A true Renaissance man, missionary Edward T. Bailey arrived in 1837 and went on to build and operate his own wheat and sugar mill and to manage newly formed Wailuku Sugar Co. A poet, painter and natural historian, he also helped native Hawaiians file land claims under the kingdom's land distribution program, directed the construction of roads and bridges in and around Wailuku, and even helped organize a smallpox inoculation program. Here he strolls the grounds of the Bailey House not long before moving back to California in 1885.

Wailuku Agribusiness

⭐ Bailey House

Edward Bailey poses with his family ca. 1840. Bailey joined the early mission school, built in 1833, as principal of the newly organized Central Female Boarding Seminary. The building later saw duty as Civil Defense headquarters during World War II. Today the Bailey House is a charming museum of Hawaiiana and missionary history operated by the Maui Historical Society. *Maui Historical Society*

"Auntie Rose" of Wailuku

That stately grey house opposite the Grand Hotel in Wailuku, residence of 81-year-old "Auntie Rose" Kepoikai, was formerly mistaken many times by out-of-towners for a hotel. Now a large plate at the gate claims it to be a "PRIVATE RESIDENCE" and strangers no longer come barging into the house asking "Where's the bar?"

This fine old house — one of the landmarks of Maui — is one of the best preserved residences on this island. Inside, it is filled with traditional, rare furnishings, and outside, its flower gardens and plants enhance its appearance.

The house was built by Awaenoa (*sic*) N. Kepoikai, one of the grand old men of Maui history, on the site of his previous home. At that time, Wailuku had only dirt roads and wooden sidewalks. An irrigation reservoir was located on the present site of the Grand Hotel, and cane fields extended on that side of Main Street as far as the Sandhills.

Nicholas Longworth and Alice Roosevelt were entertained at the Kepoikai home…and many other famous persons. Kepoikai, who died in 1911, was one of the most intellectual and advanced Hawaiians ever born on Maui. He could trace his lineage back beyond the days of Kamehameha the Great. Educated at Lahainaluna, he became an attorney, and held various posts such as Territory treasurer, Circuit Judge (to which he was appointed by Queen Liliuokalani, and later by the president of the U.S. after Hawaii became a territory), and delegate to the Republican National Convention in 1900…

Mrs. Rose Kepoikai, or "Auntie Rose" as she is called by her friends, always wears a holoku, as in the days of old Hawaii. Ancient koa tables, calabashes, poi bowls and other items fill the rooms, also some archaic Chinese teakwood furniture and many fine old dishes.

Auntie Rose is still an alert, splendid old lady. She thinks it "Too bad that all the old noted Hawaiians are dead. There are so few pure Hawaiians left now, and they don't seem to remember their great history of the past, and they forgot their language." Mrs. Kepoikai herself is three-fourths white and only one-fourth Hawaiian, but was brought up in the old traditions of the Islands.

— *Columnist Karl Wray, "Valley Isle Views," Maui News, September 1, 1945*

⭐28 Judge Kepoikai's Residence

This turn-of-the-century home at Main and Church was a true showcase of old Wailuku.
It was built and occupied by Judge Auwae Noa Kepoikai and his wife Rose, whose large collection of Hawaiiana included rare calabashes, *kāhili* and many other priceless artifacts, several of which can be seen today in the Maui Historical Society's Bailey House Museum. This location is now the site of the service station at the northeast corner of Main and Church. *Maui Historical Society*

🎰 Waikapū

Located south of Wailuku along Honoapiʻilani Highway is the rural hamlet of Waikapū, photographed here in the 1890s. In 1862 sugar growers William Cornwell and James Louzada formed Waikapu Plantation, which passed through several hands before its acquisition by Wailuku Sugar Co. in 1894. Hawaii's first artesian well outside Oʻahu was drilled here in 1881. Today the little bedroom community of Waikapū is also the home of Maui Tropical Plantation, a popular visitor attraction built around a sugar plantation theme. *Maui Historical Society*

CHAPTER SEVEN
On the Edge of Town

"Boomlet On In Colorful Iao Valley"

Away up in Iao Valley, two and a quarter miles from Wailuku, there is a miniature building boom in progress.

John G. Duarte, who has built some 20 homes on Maui, as well as the Haleakala Hotel, is making good use of his acre tract and has begun the construction of two units of six cottages he has planned and two large lodges... The larger lodge will have a dance floor and restaurant. Each cottage will be furnished complete with ice boxes, stoves and twin beds, with complete equipment of utensils for the kitchen.

The location is just above the old bridge, and right on the old battleground...

— *Maui News, November 29, 1947*

Before the war, my father started building a big house made of river rock up there, with a chapel and a hospital room—he said that way he wouldn't even have to leave home when he got sick! But there was a moratorium on new construction during the war and he only got as far as the foundation, which was also made from the river rock. After the war he built those cottages nearby, where visitors could stay and go hiking up into the valley.

Later he and my husband and I built the Hotel Iao Needle Hotel on that old foundation. We started with the restaurant and bar, opened the 17 rooms shortly after that and ran it until 1963. The restaurant was popular with local people, because it was such a hideaway. It was always interesting to see who was getting cozy together over lunch!

I like the Hawai'i Nature Center there today, because it helps return the place to nature.

— *Adelaide Rowland, John Duarte's daughter*

72 Hotel Iao Needle

Between 1910 and 1916 Maui Hotel owner W.H. Field operated an annex called Kapaniwai (*sic*) at the site of the Battle of Kepaniwai. Field later razed the annex to make way for a more modern hotel, which was never built. In 1958 the Hotel Iao Needle opened on the site, seen here shortly after its debut. The inn operated as a hotel and later a restaurant into the 1980s. Since 1991 the Hawai'i Nature Center has attracted a new generation of visitors with hands-on interpretive features in and around the old hotel building. *Adelaide Rowland Collection*

72 'Īao Valley

Sightseers pause above 'Īao Stream ca. 1930. With its deep green gorge framing 2,250-foot 'Īao Needle, the valley has long been a major Maui visitor draw. Mark Twain wrote glowingly of the area, which turn-of-the-century promotional literature then touted as the "Yosemite of Hawai'i." In Hawaiian history 'Īao Valley is best known for the 1790 Battle of Kepaniwai, in which the army of Big Island invader Kamehameha, armed with muskets, defeated the forces of Maui chief Kahekili in and around the site of today's Kepaniwai Park. *Hawai'i State Archives*

🏁73 Waiehu Beach Road

Before the Waiehu Beach Road bridge was built over ʻĪao Stream in the 1960s, crossing the stream
during periods of heavy rainfall was difficult at best. Here motorists confront the washed-out roadway ca. 1940.
This ford was located just *makai* of the current bridge.

Wailuku Agribusiness

74 Paukūkalo

Wailuku meets the sea at Paukūkalo, a homestead community near Kahului Harbor. On May 23, 1960, the sea met Paukūkalo in the form of a massive tsunami that engulfed Maui's coastal areas in the early morning hours. At Paukūkalo, the rising waters damaged homes and many other structures, including Maui Dry Good's Jobbing Department, the Takahashi Vegetable Store, the Wailuku Sugar Co. pavilion and the Full Gospel Church. Here a poi dog awaits the return of his owners at a demolished oceanfront home. *Ted Yoshizawa/Maui Historical Society*

Resources

Bartholomew, Gail (ed.), *The Index to the Maui News*, 1900-1932, Wailuku: Maui Historical Society, 1985.

Bartholomew, Gail (ed.), *The Index to the Maui News*, 1933-1950, Wailuku: Maui Historical Society, 1991.

Bartholomew, Gail, and Bren Bailey, *Maui Remembers: A Local History*, Honolulu: Mutual Publishing, 1994.

Duensing, Dawn E., *Historic Architectural Survey of Wailuku, Maui, Hawai'i*, Wailuku: County of Maui, 1993.

Johnson, Jeanne Booth, *Three Horses and a Dream*, Wailuku: MDG Supply, 1988.

Lenzer, Sara, *Maui Electric Company: 75 Years of Service*, Honolulu: Hawaiian Electric Co., 1996.

Maui News, Kahului: Maui News Publishing Co.

Nakano, Jiro, *Kanda Home: Biography of Shigefusa and Sue Kanda*, Wailuku: Iao Congregational Church, 1996.

100 Years Remembered: 1883-1983, Wailuku: St. Anthony Schools, 1983.

Pukui, Mary Kawena, Samuel H. Elbert, and Esther T. Mookini; *Place Names of Hawai'i*, Honolulu: University of Hawai'i Press, 1974.

The Bank of Maui, Ltd., Wailuku: Bank of Maui, 1919.

Wailuku Hongwanji Mission Centennial Celebration, Wailuku, 1999.

Wailuku Sugar Company Centennial, Wailuku, 1962.

Wilmington, John III, Susan Wirtz, and Richard P. Wirtz, *A History of the Church of the Good Shepherd*, Wailuku: Church of the Good Shepherd, 1988.

Index